Tate Olszewski Book Store.

Tate Olszewski Book Store

Proudly Presents!!!!

Tate Olszewski Book Store.

Chapter One: Streets To Millions!

Tate Olszewski Book Store.

"What if I told You that I could make you're company millions of dollars? You would probably want to see proof of that before you truly believe me right? To make sure that I am not just talking big numbers & that I am actually able to stay true to my words? Am I correct about that? I am guessing so...."

"It is natural for people to doubt such statements when they hear them until they see it all with their own eyes! The structure & infrastructure that makes it all work! The secrets that allow me to keep true to my words!"

"The truth is that yes in fact within minutes... I can make companies much more wealthy than they ever were prior to meeting with me even just one time!"

"I will go into detail about that a little more as we progress forward. But 1st there are some things you should know about the background of how it came to be that I could make such claims confidently & honestly & stay true to my words."

"One: July 2nd 2019 I was Injured while @ work. What I am about to reveal to you, I am confident certainly was possible to achieve before the date of my accident at work.

"Two: Anybody that attempts this gauntlet does have the ability to generate massive amounts of wealth very quickly!

"Still uncertain as to whether to believe me or not?"

"Let me show you how it is all done & We can go through it together? There is a lot of information so we will take it one step at a time. Let's proceed shall we?"

Tate Olszewski Book Store.

Chapter Two: Numbers

Tate Olszewski Book Store.

"Let's start with some key terms, words that are pretty relevant to what I am about to tell you..."

"Royalties are what a person gets paid so to speak... Every sale generates revenue, which in less technical words is making money! The more sales the more royalties."

"Example a 10% royalty earned on a single 100$ sale equals a 10$ earned royalty for who ever it is that worked to earn it!"

"Next, manufacturing costs. These are expenses related to producing a product that can be legally sold."

"Lastly for the moment, Net profits... The amount of money / revenue gained."

"Now that we all have an idea as to the meaning of these words & the underlying math that determines the profits..."

"Manufacturing expenses vary from the materials that are used in the design, to the assembly of finished products. This expense directly relates to amount of total profits! The larger the gap between the two, generally the better! Lower manufacturing costs leads to a more profits!"

"Retail sales totaling 100$ with a 70% royalty earns 70$ if there is a manufacturing cost of 10$ on that same 100$ retail sale the net profits will then total 60$ etc."

"This example that I just talked a little about is similar to the general concept of how I make can make all of the businesses their millions! Simply with honest sales & services. There is a path to success if we work towards it!"

Tate Olszewski Book Store.

Chapter Three: Business Licenses

Tate Olszewski Book Store.

"So to tell you a little about business licenses I would like to start by saying, having these in order as required definitely helps to ensure everything flows smoothly in the business world! & that there truly are a tremendous amount of resources out there to assist people with the process!"

"I in fact do have mine in order, as you can all clearly see!"

"Business licenses range greatly internationally & even here locally too!"

"Companies that are International often require a distinct type of license, separate from what a local-only business may require etc…"

"Having the proper licenses can help companies avoid problems, plain & simple!"

"I personally do business in 27 countries! I acquired the international licensing needed for me to work legally in each of those places!"

"Aside from international licenses companies may be regulated where they may also require federal, provincial / state, & municipal / city specific licenses as well."

"I have all of the required licenses as stated previously & can assure you that having all of these in order can help to ensure success!"

"There may also be other requirements that businesses must adhere to & maintain compliance with, such as taxes, & by-laws among many possible others!"

Tate Olszewski Book Store.

Chapter Four: Services Earning The Big Money Pay Days

Tate Olszewski Book Store.

"Providing quality service & products to the international & local markets can definitely go a long way towards any business having success & prospering towards vast wealth!"

"I provide many products & services! To be more specific, I provide only the best quality products & services!"

"Every product that I manufacture is world class & simply among the best ever put to market! Every service I provide has the dedication behind it to excel beyond the status quo!"

"That day back in July when I was injured on the job-site I knew instantly that I would need to consider possibly seeking a new career & that if I was going to be Successful, that I needed to elevate myself above the rest!"

"I needed to provide for people who rely on me, there was no option to fail for me! I had to succeed!"

"So I opened an independent publishing company & self-published my own books! Not just that though, I networked with other authors to publish their work & to also bring their books to market as well, not just my own! Now they pay me royalties on sales of their work in retail environments including those outside of my own store!"

"I swept the market producing high quality products industry-wide! My own brand, a unique franchise that could not only compete with the mega-corps, but out perform them!"

"I put books of many different genres to market legally at lower manufacturing costs than my competition!"

Tate Olszewski Book Store.

Chapter Five: Up-selling & Other Features /Services.

Tate Olszewski Book Store.

" As I mentioned earlier, you can check the Amazon website to verify that I am in fact an independent publisher that does put my own & other author's work to market."

"This is not all I do though! I said I could generate millions & I meant it!"

"I don't just publish books & assist in putting them to market, I do also have my own retail store where I sell Exquisite more above the normal market finds like personally signed author edition books among many other things!"

"I also sell the books not just in physical copies, but also in an online digital form that can be downloaded in its entirety to various devices such as cell phones & tablets /e-readers!"

"This sometimes requires editing, which is another service that I provide!"

"Along with editing I also have the ability to produce custom prints that's are personally signed by the author of the customers choosing or designed to the customer specifications! Which retail for an additional fee aside from the books retail value!"

"I do publishing, printing & marketing! I am more than just an author I am more than just an entrepreneur, I can make people / companies millions!"

"I manufacture product, I market it both conventional & unconventional ways, & I out compete my competition by introducing innovations to the market that my competition simply isn't!"

Tate Olszewski Book Store.

Chapter Six: How I Make It All Work

Tate Olszewski Book Store.

"I have access to product lines that currently are not available anywhere else! Unique items that nobody else has or sells! I have the potential for earnings!"

"When I opened my company I was injured, physically deemed disabled! That meant I had to overcome challenges while addressing doctors for my x-rays & CT scans, physiotherapy, & wsib & my union as well as the government too!"

"Personally I honestly needed what some might say is a miracle! Me, I thought I needed the industry's best! I called Wall St. in New York city USA... I was told by the 1st people that I spoke to that they would need months & I didn't have the luxury of that kind of time! So I called Amazon directly & inquired about what it would take to have the top north American stock market giants backing me..."

"Admittedly it was nerve racking on my already damaged nerve system, being a new venture full of unknowns... Something that I was new to... But I had a hidden ace in my pocket... I had the confidence knowing that I had the foundation established to support massive growth & profits!"

"To my pleasant surprise the very intimidating at the time mega retail giant monster of the global markets where amazingly pleasant to do business with! They had employees ready to help reach the ambitious goals I had been striving towards!"

"This is how I could compete in the global marketplace among the biggest of all the global stage! Amazon already had marketing, distribution & record keeping perfected!"

Tate Olszewski Book Store.

Chapter Seven: Allies In The Industry

Tate Olszewski Book Store.

"It was quite scary for me, calling mega giant CEO's while being near homeless & near bankruptcy! I won't say that there wasn't that aspect of unknowns & uncertainties…"

"But Amazon as I said earlier is truly amazing! I would later find out that Amazon currently networks with an amazing publishing company of their own, Kindle! & that they are also truly awesome as well!"

"Kindle worked with me while I was too injured to really work anywhere else! They have the massive ability to manufacture enormous mind boggling amounts of super high quality products that can be retailed legally! & they can do it all for below common market manufacturing costs!"

"This meant that I had reason to remain hopeful & ambitious! It meant that my venture wasn't a lost cause & that I really could become quite successfully established in an industry of global giants!"

"Kindle happily & quite pleasantly agreed to produce my books retailing them on Amazon!"

"I now had access to the manufacturing costs, marketing, & distribution to compete globally against any competition that I would be challenging! Amazon & Kindle had easily within minutes equaled up the industry playing field! & were happy to do so! They even brought in the help of their contacts / affiliates to help me accomplish everything with as little stress as possible! Remember I launched this venture while recovering from my near death accidental injury at the workplace where I had previously been employed with in the construction industry…"

Tate Olszewski Book Store.

Chapter Eight: Playing Ball With The Giants & Playing For Keeps

Tate Olszewski Book Store.

"Remember earlier I said that the 1st people I spoke to are currently situated on Wall St.? That is true! Austin Mc something or other 40 Wall St. I phoned them & even though I wasn't able to seal a deal with them it helped me to be prepared to talk with Amazon!"

"I knew that if the Wall St. Publishers weren't an option for me that I had to reach even further up to the even bigger giants at the top of the industry! & I was rewarded for my courage greatly as I had now acquired everything that I needed to compete in the big leagues!"

"In New York from what I understand they love baseball, & they have two professional league teams, similar to my situation at the time my notoriety wasn't that of the yank's but my new allies in the industry were certainly willing to help in creating that dynastic legacy similar to both of the New York teams! Which is exactly what I needed!"

"I now had an all-star roster working with me to help me become successful! Kindle global manufacturing at industry leading rates producing amazing quality products, Amazon global industry marketing, retail & distribution! & even companies like Facebook & such providing support as well via the creation of social media platforms on the biggest online social media websites etc... I even got Walmart to agree to produce my signature prints, advertisements such as store front posters & advertising flyers using Kodak glossy paper that is top quality as well!"

"That being said, for how scary it was for me at that time... The payout was certainly worth the risk /initiative that I took in calling them directly! I was now in business with the best!"

Tate Olszewski Book Store.

Chapter Nine: Blossoming Like A Rose

Tate Olszewski Book Store.

"Now I could truly blossom into the beautiful thriving rose that I had envisioned upon having to reconsider my career! Keep in mind that I accomplished all of this while on my injury downtime while waiting to be able to return to work with my union in the construction industry...."

"Growth is essential to any new business that is freshly starting out in the corporate world! & that statement also holds true when it comes to my company! I said I could generate millions in revenue / profits & I intend to keep to my word! I had now successfully assembled the dream team that had the ability to accomplish it all!"

"The industry's baddest most powerful entities were now going to bat for me, giving me the ability to produce exponential grow & near insanely amounts of wealth & profits!"

"I knew that every book /product that I produce which successfully made it to market would increase my share in the industry & I had very encouraging support networks courtesy of the mega giant industry leading name brands there helping me every step of the way! Even while I was spending months re-learning how to physically walk again!"

"The only thing I needed to do was reliably provide them with the high calibre content that they needed to maintain fresh & current inventory!"

"Considering that I was on doctors orders not to walk, sit, stand, bend, twist, or lift & that the union would not be sending me back to work injured as I was etc... I had all the time in the world to meet their retail merchandise needs!"

Tate Olszewski Book Store.

Chapter Ten: Luck In The Real World

Tate Olszewski Book Store.

"We all know that in today's modern business world for most new start up companies to succeed they need luck on their side! As you already know that is true with my venture also!"

" I believe that having the possibility to truly have great luck can in fact be influenced through proper diligent planning & preparations such as researching & assembling the right people for getting the job done without just approaching things fully unprepared & blindly! But ultimately that aspect of unknown uncertainty surely does still contribute to new business owners needing good luck on their side right from the start!"

"There is some luck that I had in life after my near fatal accident that I have yet to mention..."

"That being my I-phone 6s+ (rose gold w/ 32gb). Being that I couldn't do much else at the time other than rely on the approximately 4"x 6" device to help get me through to financial stability once again... My I-phone reliably was more than up to the challenge! Being injured with access to only very limited funds, I knew that if I could keep my phone running than I had the ability to contact the people / places that I would need to in order to make it all work! Like when I directly called the Wall St. Publisher & later Amazon shortly right afterwards! That I could connect with the outside business world that my newly acquired disability had been preventing me from accessing in person!"

"This luck of me having my I-phone quickly neutralized the obstacles that my being disabled presented rather easily & reliably as I could now easily write, edit & produce my work!"

Tate Olszewski Book Store.

Chapter Eleven: Assets

Tate Olszewski Book Store.

"My company now having its dream team all star roster supplying everything necessary for me to reach success now was only missing one crucial element... Actually having physical inventory!"

"Finding myself newly disabled, this presented unique challenges that thankfully my courage in reaching out to network with others via I-phone who were already in established positions to assist in my extremely ambitious venture had luckily paid off majorly, many ways that enabled me to bypass the obstacles that challenged my path to success..."

"One of them being that Walmart is almost always located in public transportation accessible areas of most cities! I was able to although still disabled, make my way into a Walmart store to have them print the professionally made new advertisements for my store & products at very reasonable & competitive rates!"

"Every dollar that I spent did lower the total amount of money that I had. It also was instantly converted into company advertising assets increasing the upper net value of my company as a whole. Every 2$ - 4$ printed ad increased the net value my company holds in physical inventory or stock! Even with my limited finances I was able to one print at a time print by print begin to build my business's worth! Thanks to Kindle I am easily able to beat my competition's manufacturing costs! Giving me the competitive advantage. All while reliably & consistently producing world class products! Thanks to Amazon I smoke the competitors marketing & distribution capability! I bring giants to the table in my business negotiations! That is how I make millions!"

Tate Olszewski Book Store.

The End.

www.ingramcontent.com/pod-product-compliance
Lightning Source LLC
Chambersburg PA
CBHW070847220526
45466CB00002B/912